LOVE

&

SELECTED POEMS

by

A HARON S HABTAI

LOVE

&

SELECTED POEMS

by

AHARON SHABTAI

Translated from the Hebrew by Peter Cole

The Sheep Meadow Press
Riverdale-on-Hudson, New York

All inquiries and permission requests should be addressed to:
The Sheep Meadow Press
PO Box 1345
Riverdale-on-Hudson, NY 10471

Designed and typeset by S.M.

Printed on acid-free paper in the United States. This book meets the guidelines for permanence and durability of the Committee on Production Guidelines for Book Longevity of the Council on Library Resources.

Library of Congress Cataloging-in-Publication Data

Shabtai, Aharon
    [Poems. English. Selections]
    Love and Selected Poems / by Aharon Shabtai; translated from the Hebrew by Peter Cole.
          p.   cm.
    Includes bibliographical references.
    ISBN 1-878818-53-8 (hardcover)
    1. Love poetry, Hebrew—Translations into English.
    2. Shabtai, Aharon--Translations into English. I. Cole, Peter, 1941– II. Title
PJ5054.S264A25   1997
892.4' 16--dc21   97-5231
                                            CIP
                                           r97

ACKNOWLEDGMENTS

Some of these translations were first printed in the following magazines: *The Agni Review, Scripsi* (Australia), *The American Poetry Review, Pequod, The Poems: International Poets' Festival, Jerusalem 1995* and *Modern Hebrew Literature.*

The translator wishes to acknowledge support from the Institute for the Translation of Hebrew Literature.

The poems in this book are selected from the following books: *Kibbutz and Teachers' Room*, Hakibbutz HaMe'uchad, 1973; *Domestic Poem*, Siman Kriyah, 1976; *Begin*, Keter, 1986; *Love*, AmOved, 1986; *Ziva*, Mossad Bialik, 1988; *Divorce*, Zmora, Bitan, 1990; *Metazivika*, Zmora, Bitan, 1992; *The Heart*, HaKibbutz HaMe'uchad, 1995

TABLE OF CONTENTS

INTRODUCTION

In the mid-1980s Aharon Shabtai delivered a series of radio lectures on the history of Greek drama for Israel's Open University. The deep projective rasp of his voice, the cadence of alarm, the mysterious compression of thought—all converged in my listening to form a kind of hybrid signal: half-colonel, half-oracle. Loudly turning the pages so as to lose neither precious seconds nor thrust, Shabtai hurtled through his prose, crashing through the final word of his installment just as the station cut away. The programs were taut with an intensity usually reserved for poetry, the notions proffered unsettling. Phrase by phrase, leap by leap, it was a lesson in art and worth.

I mention these lectures, the least of Shabtai's considerable opus, because a similar impression emerges from the sequence of poems at hand. Against the background both of Shabtai's previous publication and the reader's expectations of verse, there is something disconcertingly full-blown and wind-in-the-sails dramatic about *Love*. It disconcerts because we've come to anticipate from poetry in English something either subtler in its voicings or much more identifiably barbaric or documentary in its yawp, while *Love* presents the poet-protagonist center-stage, and theatrically charged, as "a kind of Aharon Eichmann," a man

who murdered love
simply

with his own two hands

took
and snapped its neck
    like a lamb ...

More than any other single component of his poetics, Shabtai's rhetoric announces his difference. Thespian in its projection, and reminiscent of Pindar's blustering sublime, it is studded with fulcral *so*s, *although*s, and *on the one hand*s. His use of these connectives is analogous to the way joints function in the body, again along Pindaric lines, in the athlete's body, the body of someone "contending for a prize": it allows for minute adjustment while bearing up under great extension and pressure. It highlights speech's texture and progression, rather than the isolated visual effect.

From Pindar also comes Shabtai's practice of mythological substitution, a method whose burden unravels the best of many a lesser poet's designs. Like Pindar, Shabtai invariably and musically locates a personal situation in a mythological context, alongside, that is, related stories, and often as counterpoint. Again the stress is on motion, or possible relation. An ideal is posited with utter conviction, but only as alternative to another ideal, or the myth-threatening real, and the essential and unstable nature of fictional creation is embodied in the pulse of the verse. The gods, in other words, are present and accounted for.

Distinctly Hebraic, Shabtai's Hellenism derives from a long and complicated history of Greek–Jewish proximity, one that runs from Greek-theater-going Philo to Rabban Gamaliel II's five hundred students of Greek wisdom at Yavneh and the Talmudic Rabbi Elisha ben Avuyah's love of Greek song (which *Hagigah* 15b tells us "never ceased from his mouth"); from the high-priest Jason's establishment of a polis and gymnasium in Antiochia-at-Jerusalem on through the Greco-Arabic nexus of medieval Hebrew Spain and, eventually, the nineteenth-century Jewish Enlightenment movement, or Haskalah. Throughout Shabtai's work, the Hellenic elements are combined with echoes of rabbinic conventions, many of which the poet turns on their heads, making, for instance, deadpan use of Talmudic rhetorical strategies, or sending the lyric expectation of the reader into the narrative maze of midrashic possibility.[1]

What Shabtai does not do, however, is use the Greek and Hebrew components to invoke authority, or dress up thought. The product of some thirty years' engagement with his several registers and texts, his characters and stories, Shabtai's Hellenism involves less a reaching-for-precedent than a drawing of his own poetic blood. His use of classical literature runs through the most passionate turns in his work and, in itself, as conduit for the vulgar (the extension of the actual) and its transformation, constitutes one of his deeper themes. Accordingly, the poet elects himself to the "severe, sublime, and wisest order of Pindar and Alighieri," but he enters with his fool's cap and Aristophanean bluntness and bite:

> Half the night
> I can't fall asleep
>
> (from desire)
> my balls are sore
>
> but I won't beat off
>
> thinking of Ixion
>
> who Zeus forgave
> and took up
>
> into the sky
> where he fell
> in love with Hera,
>
> was deceived
> and inseminated

---

[1] Midrash is most generally defined as the traditional body of commentaries on the Old Testament, dating from the fourth to the twelfth century. The term can also be used more freely to refer to any kind of contemporary commentary on the biblical text.

the goddess—

it was only a cloud

and in the end
he was bound to a wheel

for all eternity

like me
bound to the wheel
       of thinking—

bound to your name.

Lines like these, with their vigor and flair, speak for the poem as a whole and involve a development of the more static, if no less ironic, classicism of the poet's earlier work. Prior to the Hebrew publication of *Love* in 1987, Shabtai was known in Israel as a distinguished translator of Greek tragedy; a charismatic teacher of theater; and the author of two spare, objectivist collections of verse (*Teachers' Room,* and *Kibbutz*), several book-length poems grouped under the title *The Domestic Poem* (1974-87), and, in many ways the most surprising of all, *Begin,* a midrash on two pages of *The Revolt,* Menahem Begin's autobiography. The serial fragments of these books are anchored in the ideal concretion of the Greek lyricists, and they go about building a myth of The Household with comic defiance:

I read a poem by
Alcman on cheese

I, too, will write
a poem about cheese ...

As Gabriel Levin observed in a rich essay on Shabtai, "What Different Things Link Up?: Hellenism in Contemporary Hebrew

Poetry,"[2] Shabtai's early work was all about *ethos*, or right relation to, and within, the fabric of words and work and the world, about "rousing the inanimate into life...," whether that involves "an orange crate or a fragment of Archilocus." Osip Mandelstam described this approach in a different context as

> an earthenware pot, or tongs, a milk jug, kitchen utensils, dishes; it is everything which surrounds the body.... Hellenism is the conscious surrounding of man with domestic utensils instead of impersonal objects; the transformation of impersonal objects into domestic utensils, and the humanizing and warming of the surrounding world with the most delicate teleological warmth. Hellenism is any kind of stove near which a man sits, treasuring its heat as something akin to his own internal body.

Shabtai:

> I see
> a piece of furniture
>
> a packed cupboard
>
> in fact a simple
>
> painted wooden crate
> called a cupboard
>
> a piece of furniture
>
>
> 5.
> and placed in the kitchen
>
> facing
> an identical piece

---

[2] *Prooftexts* 5 (1985). Levin traces the Hellenic elements in the poetry of Saul Tchernikovsky, Harold Schimmel, and Shabtai, noting how these elements were involved in the transformation of the language, landscape, and literature of the Holy Land.

I think
the kitchen contains

an Eden

of wisdom

6.
Wisdom nests
in fire and salt

The water supply
is mythological ...
                    (*The Domestic Poem*)

This is Shabtai circa 1976, the young father. Ten years later
Love appears to involve a total rejection of *The Domestic Poem*'s ethic
in favor of a new poetic whose volatility is "threatening to bring about
marvelous changes." Gone, it seems, is the moral magic of the object,
the democracy of substance. The heat of Mandelstam's stove is no
longer "akin" to that of "his own internal body." In fact, Shabtai in
Love is still very much a poet of the ideal, though now it resists his
naming, its ethos less manageable:

I don't want
always to be

a friend to a chair,

nor the philosopher
of the chair

but myself
a chair of flesh and blood ...

Having devoted his life as poet-husband-father to establishing in mock pre-Socratic fashion the political centrality of the family, Shabtai finds himself suddenly destroying what he has become, changing ideals, "choosing new gods." Uncertain of who he is, at least in relation to who he was, and, as is almost always the case with each of us as potential hero, vulnerable and perhaps guilty within that uncertainty, he finds himself driven, or possessed, which is to say, daemonic:

> My hands are good—
>   erotic—
> in the ancient sense,
> the daemonic ...

But driven where? And possessed by what?

The narrative informs us that D., an old flame, is the shadow presence behind his story. Some twenty years earlier he had known her and missed his chance. Now the ghost of that murdered love returns to haunt him. The poet, author of *The Domestic Poem*, married and the father of six, falls in love and pursues his hope from the past, his chance for deliverance. And though he resents it, he quickly comes to recognize the fantastic, narcissistic nature of his quest. While he very much wants D. and the new life she implies, Shabtai is aware that something else is being worked out:

> From here on in I know I'll wail
> like a hound
> lying on the doormat
> (on my back)
> licking my thing
>
> I'm becoming
> from day to day more of an idiot
>
> putting, for Christ's sake,
> all sorts of garbage into my mouth
>
> in order to bring up

the Muses's
    roses

using love

in order to enter the shit
more deeply ...

Readers familiar with Shabtai's career might recall at this point that one of the volumes of *The Domestic Poem* was elegantly titled *Shit/Death*, and that the theme is familiar: the way up, to fullness, is the way down, through defilement and death. A few sections later *Love*'s Moirai exhort the poet "to look for [his] love in the grave." And the poem has barely begun. Far from being a book about unrequited longing, or two people getting together, or a couple failing to stay together, *Love* is as much a journey into Shabtai's sense of his own thwarted vitality (read: mortality) and his power to kill as it is a kind of commentary on his "back pocket" collection of scrolls: "Lamentations and Ruth, the Song of Songs, and so on"—the metrical etcetera accounting for the wisdom literature of Ecclesiastes and the deadly reversals-in-love of the Book of Esther.

Not surprisingly, halfway or so into the poem it becomes evident that the quest for D. will fail; that D. isn't much more than a thought in the poet's mind; that in fact it is the poet's own past (the death he holds) that drives the agon forward. From here the poem moves in the direction of uneasy expiation, of transforming the Furies into Eumenides. Desire persists, as the "Additional Poems" recapitulate the crisis ("I'd like to touch you, it would be splendid to touch a thought"), and we begin to understand that *Love* is illuminating the eros of the incessant collapse and reconstruction of one's world, along an arc of potentially shared passion and understanding. Failure and success in that process are for love-stories proper, and *Love* itself contains a wild one. But the book as a whole tells of the destructive-constructive nature of those stories, and of the painful, particle-cloud-like physics of self.

All of this was new territory for Hebrew poetry in the mid- eighties, and it established Shabtai as a major voice on the Israeli scene, in many ways the rogue successor to European-born Yehuda Amichai and Natan Zach, generally regarded as the most important of the Hebrew poets who came into their own in the fifties and the sixties. Shabtai inherited the no-nonsense diction of Amichai, the early minimalism and off-center detail of Zach, but from the outset he was defining a different Israel, articulating a newer music, a Hebrew "free of ambiguity," stripped down and objective before physical fact and abstraction alike. In terms of foreign influence there was more Williams and Olson than Auden, more Ponge than Rilke or Trakl.

Love involves a further extension of that dictional ethos, with several twists. The plainness remains, alongside the scatological register. The visual contours are well defined, and the quality of the line is superior. There is, however, an overall lift and emotional dimension that is new to the work, an elaboration, perhaps, of the extended midrash on Begin's paternalistic affection for the people. The Hebrew of *Love* is fast and tightly woven, dense with inconspicuous links and yet clear, quick in its pivot and capable of tremendous elevation and range. It draws our attention to daily speech and takes that speech through astonishing vaults and into peculiar abutments. It can manage a carnivalistic lewdness beside sublime rumination; soaring lyric en route to satire of self; clownish comedy within a subversive rhetoric of flux; the epyllionic gesture and the rhythms of the narrative swell.

The English translation here makes every effort to reflect these qualities. There has been nothing elaborate in the transfer, though often it was best to displace certain effects from their position in the Hebrew poem, and inevitably a share of the humor was spilled in that shift. More complicated was the problem of Hebrew's relation to itself, of the poem's treatment of Hebrew texts and the tradition of word games that characterize so much of biblical and postbiblical literature. Shabtai plays with the letters of his language, puts his lover's initial (*D.*) into the pronoun I (*ani*) and gets God (*adonai*). He breaks down the word "love" (*ahavah*), letter by letter, and finds it composed of the first Hebrew letters of the words "God" (*elohim*), "The Name" (an epithet for God—*HaShem*), "covenant" (*brit*), and again "The Name" (*HaShem*). Some of this is possible to recreate in English without surrendering too much in the way of comprehension and drive.

Nevertheless, there are obvious problems that readers without Hebrew will note. For one, the Hebrew letters do not always have consistent English equivalents. (The letter *aleph* in *ahabah* is vocalized differently and pronounced "e" in the word for "God"—*elohim*; the letter *bet* in *ahabah* is soft, and pronounced "v", but in *brit* ("covenant") the "b" is hard.) My solution here has been to maintain the play by incorporating both the translation and transliteration of these key terms into the rhythm of the sequence. Readers can always go back and work out the logic of a live passage, but if the underlying music of a poem in translation is lost, so is the poem, and the reader, and nothing in footnotes or theory will find them.

In the decade since publishing *Love*, Shabtai's output has been staggering. He has published some fourteen volumes of Greek drama in translation, complete with annotation and appendices of related lyric poetry also in his own translation, and, from the English, a translation of Middleton and Rowley's *The Changeling*. (The critic Yoram Bronofsky has called Shabtai's translation of Greek drama the most important project now underway in Hebrew literature.) And he has ventured into new poetic territory, including that of the English metaphysicals and the sonnet. Four books have appeared, *Divorce, Ziva, Metazivika,* and *The Heart,* and his new poems, with their rough-cut, formal mix of reflection and smut, turn up regularly in the weekend literary supplements, frequently to a chorus of objections and Sabbath tskks.

 This latest metamorphosis of Shabtai's again breaks new Hebrew ground, and even readers who disapprove of the ribald nature of the work and its seemingly reactionary formal tack admit that the man is one of the very few writers engaged in the revitalization of the national poetic registers. Shock value apart, this is something Shabtai has been doing from the outset. Much of the pleasure, for example, in his first signature-style book, *Kibbutz,* is bound up in the simple delight the poet takes in using the modern and still-new Hebrew names of things:

> I like the potato
> peeler

the bread slicer

and the two huge pots with the steering
wheels on the side

the storeroom for crates

I like the kitchen in its entirety

including the loading dock's concrete floor ...

Where another Levantine poet engaging in cultural retrieval, George Seferis, obsessively and somewhat nostalgically sought a new Hellenism in his wanderings, conjuring images of Homer's King of Asine, "sometimes touching with our fingers his touch upon the stones," the young Shabtai declares, two decades into the State of Israel's existence:

Our culture's contained in a few
tools and their objects—
i.e., a straw broom,
a chisel,
a pitchfork and scoop
caustic soda
for the calves' horns,
a rubber pipe, a glass
tube and inseminator's glove ...

The flatness of the verse's surface notwithstanding, the tension and technical reach of the listing in this early work conducts an undertone of the Haskalah call for a widening of Hebrew literature's sights. (Writing of the nineteenth-century prose writer Peretz Smolenskin, Eliezar Ben Yehuda, the father of modern Hebrew and compiler of its multi-volume lexicon, asks: "Have any of [his] readers ever felt that in all of the circumstances of the different events that this very capable author brought into his stories, he never once mentioned, for example, the simple, the common act of tickling? This act which we meet often in every story in a living language we will never meet in the stories of Smolenskin, simply because he did not have a word for it.... Whoever wishes to write something of wisdom and science, and especially someone like myself who speaks Hebrew at home with the children, about everything in life, feels every moment a lack of words without which living speech cannot take place.")

At the same time, the basic impulse of the poem brings to mind Ben Yehuda's linking the linguistic revival of Hebrew with the people's agricultural rebirth. And one detects in the poem's tonal pitch a subtle echo of the highly compact, straightforward Hebrew of the Mishnah, with its code of laws relating to agriculture and health, marriage, women and holy things—a return, as it were, of the basics:

> Wheat and tares
> are not [considered] diverse kinds with one another.
> Barley and two-rowed barley,
> rice wheat and spelt,
> a broad bean and a French vetch,
> a red grasspea and a grasspea,
> and a hyacinth bean and a Nile cowpea,
> are not [considered] diverse kinds with one another ...
> (*Mishnah, Kilayim 1:1, trans. Irving Mandelbaum*)

Lest this carbon-dating approach to Shabtai's Hebrew seem remote from the poem's emotional emphases, one might recall that the first "Hebrew-speaking family" was rather artificially established in Jerusalem only in 1881, with the polyglot Ben Yehuda's announcement to his Russian and Yiddish-speaking wife that henceforth only Hebrew would be allowed at home; and the first child was born into that linguistic hothouse a year later. Prior to this there were of course Hebrew speakers (the complex history of religious and secular Hebrew literature looming large in the background) but Hebrew had not been the spoken language of a given place for over two thousand years. And only with Ben Yehuda and the modern Hebrew movement did the vernacular literature begin to take shape, in the context of poetry with a series of formal rebellions—beginning with Avraham Shlonsky and Natan Alterman and continuing through Amir Gilboa, Amichai,

Zach, Avot Yeshurun, and the generation of David Avidan, Shabtai, Harold Schimmel and Yona Wallach. So while the stylistic distance travelled by Shabtai over the course of his career is considerable, the farm inventory of *Kibbutz* in fact evolves quite naturally into the sexual and affective mapping of *Metazivika*:

> With each passing season and year
>   the heart descends more toward the rear;
> with the cock and in the moistened hole,
>   it battles the angel.
>
> Between the legs it gradually lessens
>   the distance from Rome to Jerusalem ...

And the extravagant irreverence of *The Heart*'s thirty-two sonnets (with "32" being the numerological equivalent of "heart," thus "A Heart of Sonnets") is, in a historical light, revealed as the most central of Hebraic concerns:

> I look at the Prime Minister's face and remember
> how cold and hard the wooden seat of the toilet
> was during the days of the British Mandate ...
> Now, two whores, nationalism and religion
>
> have taken over the country and made a pact
> to turn the heart's pasture into a shithouse
> and pluck the feathers of Hebrew culture.
> A man wakes, and refuses to look in the mirror.
>
> I see three old women, Rebecca, Rachel and Sarah,
> in a soup kitchen passing a tooth from hand to hand;
> only a little meat is left on the carcass
>
> of that sweet bird that once sang in the window
> from its high branch. Chew slowly, hags, the cupboard's bare,
> and soon the Hebrew poem will have to blast from the ass.

This isn't poetry for the politically correct or the meek, for the mauve décor of the suburban *shul* or Foreign Ministry brochures. Its internal landscape is closer to Menippus and Meleagros of Gadara than the Israel of anyone's news.

Peter Cole
Jerusalem, February 1996

LOVE

1986

1.

I'm a man
who murdered love

simply
with his own two hands

took
and snapped its neck
     like a lamb

and then, with his fee,
his slaughterer's fee,

promptly turned
into

a *groisser hocham*
—a wise ass—

wise at night
and wise on his ass

—and so

there's Cain and there's Abel
and Joseph and Deborah
and Hamor the Shechemite

and finally

a kind of Aharon Eichmann

wandering around
with—stuck
in his back pocket—

all five scrolls

Lamentations and Ruth
The Song of Songs
    and so on

but waiting
for the firing squad

it's sublime

    my eyes

blinded by tears
to take the ringing
    bullets

like the 5
stars of The Bear

I pronounce

life
an act
    of suicide
The New Testament

means
die and die

I can't be
more specific

there's no one
(truly no one)

to whom I'd explain

the specifics

and whoever there is

to lend an ear
and listen

anyway
turns to nothing:

I'm sobbing
over a neck so white

—it's unbelievable,
unbelievable—

I swear
a neck as white
    as this one

has never existed

I told her:
D., even if they cut off your legs

(I called them "chips")

I'll love you

It was, in fact, a vow ...

You know how far I'd go with her?

Even into apostasy
even into the PLO

I'd—

so I told her—
plain and simple

and all night
(every night)
kiss you

and I'm
    entirely capable
I mean it in all seriousness

of carrying out
just such a total kiss

I'm a man
who, gradually,

has learned

the arts of love

I never
once betrayed my wife

(before the marriage I went
two or three times to whores)

and that's it—
afterwards
year after year

patiently I've learned

        patience

I'm able,
how should I put it,

to care for

to care for any
creature requiring care

i.e.,
I take into account

when I stare
at my beloved
the infant
the elder
(the entire design)

and the ill

which follows
from the healthy

and the foul
and the exhausting
and the recurrent

(which is to say:
    The Law)

so instead of saying

"D., look—

here's the mezuzah,

bore
the awl through my ear"

kept to the fence

year after year
I've barked and barked

at your beauty

I remember a poem
by Alcman—
on Astymeloisa:

"Astymeloisa
won't answer me"
(*ouden ameibetai*)

"but she holds a garland,

she's like a bright star
cut out of the sky"

and he adds

"like a golden bough,"
etc. (what a wonderful
        poet)

you— Astymeloisa!

my heart's broken
with saying
(entirely despite myself)

that your nipples
are like thorns

why
would nipples of thorn

suddenly shatter

a grown man's life?

  and why
didn't you listen

when I said:
D., come *with* me—

leave your husband,

for me,

a man who, from a mop,

can trick
200 golden proverbs?

Half the night
I can't fall asleep

(from desire)
my balls are sore

but I won't beat off

thinking of Ixion

whom Zeus forgave
and took up

into the sky

where he fell
in love with Hera,

was deceived,

and inseminated
   the goddess—

it was only a cloud
and in the end

he was bound to a wheel
for all eternity

like me
bound to the wheel
   of thinking—

bound to your name

2.

From here on in I know I'll wail
like a hound

lying on the doormat

(on my back)
licking my thing

I'm becoming
from day to day more of an idiot

putting, for Christ's sake,
all sorts of garbage into my mouth

in order to bring up
the Muses'
    roses

using love

in order to enter the shit
more deeply

and now I'm free
to be zero, a pig—
a pig

so as
to be a torch
    to love

so that you'll
open your gate to me

there's nothing pragmatic

about this love

and not quite having
the grounds for complaint

or quarrel,
there's nothing, as Wittgenstein put it, to say

you didn't love me enough

because I
    didn't have time
to shit on your head

because you
hadn't yet sniffed my balls

and dare I mutter

this concept "lover"

is in the end, for better or worse,
at the mercy of the concept "wife"

(though this
is house-slipper wisdom)

my fire wants something
to burn

I don't want to end up
a pathetic lecher

a hug snatched here
a blow job there

I'm a poet

a Jesuit

of the severe, sublime, and wisest order
of Pindar and Alighieri

but also
of Archilocus

who, I should add,
if it's news,

could sketch how—on Paros—
one seduces a little sister

"Let me, sweet, crawl in to you
under the gate,

I'll just play
in your grass"

and no one knew better
than he how to finish:

"I've spilled
my white power,

while my fingers
were in her golden hair"

so he would tell me
in his way

"Aharon,
it's impossible to distinguish

between words and cock!"

3.

All but all but all
        is love

but everyone eats

with his own utensils

so I shut up— here

near the window
(rain now)

in the narrow passage
between Nanno's room

and the oil tank

the dog
turds

are piling up
(piling up,
threatening
and afterwards smearing—

turning into a
muck with the ground

and all that's fine)

and because of the heaviness
        in my gait

I'm considered a kind of milkman
or dairy farmer

though one who lifts
     a sock here

a diaper there

a few stains of shit
stuck along the porcelain bowl
     of the toilet

I remove with religious simplicity
in the warm stream of my piss,

working, toiling, thinking, writing,
a kind of filthy angel,

my will's allotted as it should be,
and suddenly now I don't
have the will for a thing

but D. D. D.—

to hold you by your primal limbs

4.

I want to lie in wait for you
within these shrubs

to lie in wait and lie in wait

and, suddenly,
simply to snatch you away

helped
by that deep groove

that deep groove
which was, as it were, created
  so when it's snatched

  the hand won't slip

and then again
the entire body, your body, is smooth
        as mother-of-pearl

and the body's smooth
sevenfold smooth because it's speech

so how, pumpkin,
how will I be able to live

and how will I hold you?

5.

From an infant I've turned
into a fat man

my hair's going gray
and becoming a kind of
        useless rag

when I eat
I run my tongue

along my dentures

on the other hand
I'm awfully young, and funny,
cordial, my hands are good

erotic— in the ancient sense,
        the daemonic—

and my back is strong
despite one lousy disc

I strained
when I picked up a stone idiotically

My brother's tanned legs
(he boasted of, philandered with)
are long since eaten, whereas mine

mine are o.k.—last night I even dreamed
I was called in to play fullback

unfortunately, my scrotum's shot

(once it would shrink up in the cold
like a crop)

and my penis I admire

fascinated by its white liquid
I've learned in my life to use it wisely

and your belly is like a levelled bowl
and at its tip are leaves of laurel

6.

Within myself I've discovered
an opening

imagine for a moment the cave
of Pan at Banias

and was astonished
at the shiftings of meaning there

that what's wanting we call an opening

and the opening we call the past

that the past has the supple body
of a young woman

and she told me
what no one ever told me
(what I've always wanted to be told)

and as much as she told me
so the girl in me grew

deepening, and deepening, and deepening
the past

and, accordingly, the openness

and, as it were,
all became wanting

7.

D., you've given up
    on being released from my soul,

since it, just now, is the womb
the womb of your soul

and also because my hands embody
          the exclusive
  living science concerning your thighs

in my hands your thighs will be able to sing,
they'll recite from the Orphic Fragments

the thighs long for their missing significance:
a wanting more giant and crazier—

and that want's in the palm of my hand
this is an ancient bit of wisdom
      the Muses taught me

so let your husband go berserk—
let him draw something blunt or sharp

he's a good man, a sweet, decent guy
I know, I know, he's my lover as well

maybe he'll buy a rifle

and drop me like a sparrow
    ridiculous
  on Mt. Moriah

8.

I'm no longer ashamed to cry

and I know how to cry
sitting at night in the kitchen

(after straightening up
and everything's clean) suddenly crying

because there isn't a chance in the world
of turning the wheel

back to 1966
and the young man who turned
        and shut a door

on you in a room
with two foam-rubber mattresses
        and a sink

who can say what might have been

I took the road written out within me

I married the woman
the letters of my name spell out

but then I had my chance, in 1966,

which couldn't have been
realized till now,
in 1986, when there isn't a chance

as for love, I was an embryo then
with my wife I've learned

over the course of twenty years
how

in theory and practice
I could have loved you then

in other words
I've learned to change my name ...

(what the Moirai permit only after a thousand years

and in their guile make certain
the new name won't be revealed, except as quotation

and in quotation, the spelling the same ...)

my love for you meanwhile
has flourished like a wood

a wood where the dead are resurrected

9.

It goes now without saying
I'll die

the links between
my body and soul won't weaken

but the message will blur
and be blurred

Apollo instructed the Furies
(snake-haired, blood-fed hags)

the marriage bed— he said—
is the gift of the gods to man

and it alone is morality
rhythm, music, proportion,
and it alone

the correct language
incarnate as sinew and skin

in the body of nature and the body
            of the polis

You wouldn't marry me

and that refusal
will fluster this fragile system

of surrender and resistance
of give and take

which is my organism
which writes itself and writes itself

and words as it's worded
as it takes in life

a slow fire in which I burn
endowing, then, this sacred hearth

feeding its flames

with what the fire refuses, and so
it takes its own life, becomes negation

yielding its purity,
which burns and refines

and life itself, despite
blushing cheeks and a loud belly,

    turns to death

10.

This unrequited love
is all I have

This wanting in fact
      what *have* is

Your legs, D.,
are present within my heart—

like a goldsmith
I weigh them out on infinitesimal scales

but the word "infinitesimal"
mustn't mislead

my own legs
are more distant, more abstract

your legs more integral
to my own being

they're a sacred thing
belonging to no one

nevertheless
for me they're a cruse of water
(a certain bird brings to a prophet)

those legs are, after all,
my body
I walk on them, and fall

they grant me height
and downfall

refine me, establish
me, me
within those scales

I'm out of my mind with love

nothing in nature
matters to me

on the contrary,
I'm waiting
for a horrible earthquake

a natural disaster,
so the sky would open

so there would appear
    primeval monsters

the bears
that devoured the children

now I know what
"always" is

that a religion and hell
were created for *me*

your legs are the gospel—

I know their splendor
comes from the soul

from your soul and from mine

but let me, people, let me draw
really near them

don't take them away with words
that contradict at one

and the same time the specific example
of D.'s legs, which were taken from me

which sent down roots in my heart

legs I know how to live alongside

taking upon myself
an asceticism of loyalty and lust

observance and practice
The Well-Laid Table and conjugal rites

to establish modesty—
to stare without staring

to look without turning away
so as to come to the edge of blurring
               and blindness

on the other hand
try to see these legs as angels

these are *your* angels
Let's preserve our angels
preserve this absence—

O the legs on D.

O the legs on D.

11.

You've made me poor and forced me
to make you poor in return

and from here on in the world
will evolve as an abscess

of sexual greed— I'll
definitely manage to seduce you

I'll flatter you
I'll coax you into exposing a nipple

I'll speak to your heart
asking

to let me kiss your rear

already now I'm
changing my ideals

choosing new gods

(for I'm not going out

except so as not
            to return—

which is to say

the mode, the ethos
the place— the placing,
        word, and genius—
        are changing)

listen D.:

the gods get annoyed

they're fragments
of ourselves

and we're cosmic fragments
and other fragments
and still others

and regret's pointless
and wealth and poverty are pointless— everything's
            wealth and everything's poverty—

like an old cloth of gold
   we'll tear gods

when I put my lips to your asshole

12.

Apart from its being as an organism

the tree
is also a trap for light

and this light
is indestructible

because everything,
in the driest manner,

is only light
only light only light

and out of that light
D. takes form

her breasts are small

they're the signs
I set for myself
in order to single her out—

because flesh is script

and both of us are already written out,
each beside the other;

the permanent is only
mask to what changes

so our marriage knows no limit
no limit to lechery

try, you won't be able to find me

I don't have the head of a dog

I'm not what I am

it's convenient, then, to say
I'm actually only light

(hence my "cruelty"
"generosity" ...)

because I'm destined
to burn and shine

even if my doing so
is couched in the softer
    terms of urban existence

toward which you're retreating
at the moment, a star—

you—
refusing to be a star

13.

Body body body please,

come stretch yourself across me

let sleep
be wakefulness

and wakefulness sleep

body body

I'll worship you

I'll ready the offering:
    myself
(I don't want myself except
to offer myself)

my blood is my fate
and my fate the deep

music of your voice

I don't want
always to be

a friend to a chair,

nor the philosopher
of the chair

but myself
a chair of flesh and blood

a chair of
flesh and blood for whom?

A chair of flesh and blood for D.

A chair of flesh and blood for D.

14.

"It's convenient, then, to say I'm
    actually only light"—

that's what I said—

the light lights firstly
(on) itself

and that's the story
of how I was burned

understand—
to the man who didn't dare
   dream he might
one day touch the tip of your finger

you say
after twenty years—

You're a wonderful creature

I've always loved you

always
loved and still love;

Got it?
you told me, me

"You're a wonderful creature
I've always loved you,"

and all at once
as though with lightning—lightning

that splits the trunk of a tree
as though with lightning you seared me

and life as it is
slipped into life as it isn't

life as it isn't
  into life as it is—

but that isn't it—

what's the meaning
of that gift which fills me

filling-emptying
given and, in as much as it's given,
                taken away

and as much as it's taken away
the solace that it's given grows

and, to the extent it's given,
pride swells

in the fact that you're not alive,
that you've been torn from your life?

On the other hand—
I've built my life on despair

on faithlessness,

on lovelessness,

but, looking back,
what was all that despair

but a searching for faith?

What's despair composed of,
if not the flesh of love?

So what does it mean
(so what's it about)
this life from which, as I said,
   I've been torn—

and that (in retrospect)
in order to form it
   to find myself within it?

In anger, in love, in despair
I feel like biting your tits

I'm going wild
because I've lost you within me

How will I find your living body
within that stupendous blaze?

15.

Look, my life's already the cycle
I've sketched—

from marriage to craving
from craving to marriage

to lift up craving
and crown it with the garland
            of marriage

to revive, within the marriage,
  craving

two women are hidden
face within face
    within my soul

and beyond them a third

the third woman's calling me
to look for my love in the grave

but her speech embodies
  Sophia—Wisdom,

and the grave (the underworld) means
            the opportunity
  of Orpheus and Heracles

in short—
the refuse which is
    the food of redemption;

you didn't finish— she says—

going down in order to ascend

by the shortcut of love,

go down, down my sweetness
down my beloved

What's the heart for—
I scream—

if not
to put a brick across?

And the body—I wail—

if not in order
            to know death?

And what purpose does love
serve—I sob—if not

to wait in vain?

Go down my sweet, go down
she tells me

in every woman
you look for and find
you'll always find

only your fate—
your Moira whose name is mine: Ita

16.

D., when the time comes we'll strip:
it'll be a seminal morning

we'll realize the value of water
and thus

and nevertheless we'll wash

I'll shut my eyes
and wash your body

or better
that total secret will be
            entirely in your hands

for morality is the body—
and the best definition of body is fullness

and there is no morality within what's partial
except as body

and such a body I intend to marry

so with your fingers you'll follow the water
the water's message

into that same wondrous weft
of hollows and sockets—
    the work of God—

I'll wash too,
with a firm, exacting brush

I'll scrub the dirt
out from under my nails

I'll wash my balls
I'll wash my belly

(because
washing is a kind of barter with soul)

Once we were all— said Aristophanes
—undivided primal creatures

but Zeus split us
    and knotted
in the navel of each such miserable half
the edge of that cut

and on that morning we'll be united
again a sphere

your mother, the venerable goddess

dresses you up in a white gown
its veil's whiteness above and beyond
                    our world

so that I'm afraid
to act, to act on my love

D.,
listen to what my dream is, my every dream:

to put the ring on your finger

and the pomegranate seed in your mouth

Here are the little children
who escort the bride and groom
                on their eternal journey

Do they realize that Aharon is Hades
and D.— Persephone?

17.

You've let me taste your body's honey

I tasted it
and all at once the world was gone

in order to bring it back
(I'm obliged, it's my duty)
I'll have to forget

alright, I forget

and remembrance is a kind of forgetting
a forgetting of remembrance

forgetting—which is remembrance intensified

a forgetting—which itself
I've got to forget

Your hand, the Shechina's hand

turns into erasure

erasure erasing its eraser
and that will be my grave—

Let the world come back and feel good

18.

I wanted to elaborate—to say
that man is memory

but there's no point in saying
        what's already been said

and said in the language of the body
and said in the language of creation

and said
in the manner of man and woman

and in this light
"You've let me taste your body's honey"

is eternity

is man

naked and forgetting himself

receiving the divine honey

the honey of your hugs

the honey of your pure soul

the honey of your eyes

the honey of your knees
the honey of your back with hints of sweat

the armpit whose sign is "L"
                (Life)

the breasts (*shaddayim*) which are
the explicit name of God (*Shaddai*)

(that everything enfolds, enacts,
                 grants and opens)

Ah—
you've let me taste your body's honey

19.

I said "opens"
and my heart shudders

because
I want you opened

and the whole world
is one gigantic refusal

Satan's black
    breastplate

daily renewed
like a book's pages

the book of history,
or the laws of probability,
ethics,
    the chatter of journalism

so that the cunt, yes, the cunt
(I say it because I'm angry)

your cunt
is making fun of me

because it's clothed
in the world's understanding

and much as I seek it out

and call to it
like someone who's lost his echo
            and shadow

and call it also
   by other names:

and on the contrary, again:
         Here cunt, here cunt!

I'll get nothing

but another degree
            or maybe

an invitation to lecture

the cunt will go into hiding

so long as I say

that love is a cosmic body

that love requires
a cost of living index

a land, a port, a roof, a floor,

an entire ethos
sprouting like metaphorical mushrooms

and as long as I
   can't open you

nothing
will be able to stop me

from turning

into an expanding star
   growing richer

and therein more full
     of gaps

a star of words
   filling up with emptiness—

a man who could actually be
an ordinary husband,

and instead of killing
myself in the cunt's mockery

and losing the cunt in greed—

to stoop and perform
in the manner of Jewish males

with a well-circumcised penis

to slake my lust and even raise seed ...

the entire land, the entire land

would be reduced at last
(for man's advantage is the minimum)

to the body of a certain woman

20.

I'm a love poet

who said to his beloved
honey, you stay in bed

and I'll
go get some eggs

except that my going
has lasted twenty years

twenty years
I've been out getting eggs

though I did believe
the act most appropriate
        for a love poet

to say to his beloved
honey, you stay in bed

and I'll
go get some eggs

21.

This love, this addiction— to eggs

has cost me this—
I can't stand them any longer

I want diamonds, diamonds

diamonds big as ostrich eggs

though as I say it
I'm talking again about eggs

ach— because I know only about eggs
know, in fact, only how to hate

22.

The light's gone out in the john,
I need to get some sleep

If I drop in on you now
you'll probably be embarrassed

to be without panties

just out of the shower

and like the Delphic Oracle I'll say:

"The woman who cuts my hair tomorrow, her I'll love"

23.

I dreamed I'd gone to bed with you,
the essence of the matter dreamlike

beyond the act of it—
a rubbing of member on member

for a dream, after all, is a dream
as a star is a star

as opposed to, say, the patch of stones at hand

Your tolerant husband was there
because of him, perhaps, I didn't take off my pants

I penetrated, but wasn't free

For the Greeks the winds are gods

and I like when I couple
for the cruel north wind, Boreas,

to pass with a whistle, as if on a chariot,
    through the crack in my ass

that ass at that moment is a high hill
and the act the center of the earth, the center
                of the dictionary

all the words flee from this center
like worker-ants to the docks and markets of the world
to wait in lines, to offer alms, or gather rags

every bead of sweat from this meeting of Aharon and D.
preserved as royal jelly

in a golden bowl—a flask's elixir

like the double flask that was tied
by a golden thread to Creusa's wrist

a gift of Erichthonios in which
there were two drops of blood from the Gorgon

absolute life in one—absolute death in the other—

it's impossible to mingle the two—she tells her slave
(who was sent to poison her son

but saves them both in the end— mother and son)

because that's what good and evil are
but to keep them apart is impossible too

and they're preserved in a single bracelet
formed by the hand of Athena

just as our bodies in embrace
are a oneness that won't be united

a divided oneness, divided forever

even in the dream—for also in the dream
I wasn't permitted to flood your womb with my seed

24.

It occurred to me that instead of sleeping
                    with you
I'd sleep instead with another woman
like Leah instead of Rachel

and instead of Leah—Bilhah
(or Zilphah, I don't remember)

there's a girl like that
five streets over

I need only to bother
and climb a few flights to her rooftop apartment

and the room crowded with knickknacks and trash,
primitive musical instruments, and such,

but for one reason or another I've settled
on tempting myself with my lonesome body

and—on the other hand—on starving myself
as a lion is starved

which, rejecting a can of beans,
waits for its live prey
(a wonderful mammal like you, a woman-mare)

dying but defending the gist
of the lofty notion that a lion exists

and maybe the idea's idiotic
and a lion's only an overgrown cat

and within each woman you'll find another ...

25.

Apollo raped Creusa
(in a cave below the Acropolis):

the gods don't know what love is
because one can't refuse them

can't take, either, anything from them

in order to fall in love like me

Apollo would have had to be
a man with D., who's unattainable,

who sits shining her husband's boot,

and also to go in fear of death

nevertheless I identify
with the god

unable to marry a woman
because he's kept from all limitation

and passes through life like a violent wind
always threatening like a double

within each harmless daily act

so I'm also dying to ravish,
to ravage the human concepts
that divide in order to create
   the singular and particular
   (weakness, and within it longing,
         a kind of power ...)

I'll violate you, annihilate longing,
annihilate weakness, annihilate power

annihilate you, annihilate myself

26.

My two hands compose poems,
miles of poems,

from within your body—

remember D., the honey

in the lion's
carcass, the honey ...

the miles
jab at the sky

stab at the clouds

tickle the stars

man's such a schmuck—

a poem stuck up God's ass—

thwarted, feasting, thwarted, feasting

27.

My wife, you've forgotten that life is madness

(I'm not even done with wiping my ass
and I run to write you this—

afterwards I'll go back and finish)

for too many years you've walked
  the Milky Way

and it's obvious,
for your other name is Diana

you were, then, Diana of Ephesus
a maiden whose body is covered with nipples

and at whom the whole world sucks
and then, having done so, loathes

loathes the breast and the milk
  so as to grow

so as to separate and, as I mentioned, grow

to become a wandering hunter
in the sky like Orion ...

Nevertheless Orion seeks you

not for milk, but madness
from the goddess's beauty—

the goddess who goes mad and screams
                on the backs of mountains,
milks the lioness and curdles the whitening cheese

and she has many names:

Artemis, Aotis, Orthia, Bendis, Anahita

28.

I'm a wounded animal

the day before yesterday
in a kitchen

I stood before you and your husband

for a moment puffing
a breath of life into two statues

(which sit on their marriage
as though on a stack of wares)

but I'm happy
now that my guts are spilled

and my heart's
entirely clean of that trash

called conscience, happiness
                    and so forth

I'm exactly
what a man should be and worthy

my house is actually
          a shrub

and my people
a Scythian tribe in which
the woman and dogs
are communal

I'd sleep

under the open sky

with my horse, my bitch, and you

but first I'll need to leave
and win the trust of the animals

and afterwards, pumpkin,
I'll come back stinking
   from the wilderness

and one full night I'll lick your rear

a rear astonishingly smooth
from its thousands of hours of dancing

my balding head

wreathed with heavy garlands
of wispy grass and thistle and sage

since the day before yesterday
my heart's hung higher in my body

picture it
I feel the pulse of the blood

I've gone back
to being a beast—I'm pure

pure
and if I were tastier

I'd suggest that you and your husband
cook me and eat

29.

I'm a whore—

I shouldn't have said it

not enough people are wise
(which is why
   silence is a hedge to wisdom)

that love is freedom

the annulment of all property
(not necessarily material)

and that it's possible
to pay in counterfeit bills

I'll take out my dentures

and replace them with teeth
of silver and gold

I have no ideas or opinions

because all the ideas are mine
            (and not mine)

I haven't got words

and I *am* words

I haven't got love

and love is all I am

and I'm coupled

to the whore in you

indeed there aren't enough people sufficiently wise

to understand what that means—a whore

beyond the drabness of "social science"

so let them read
the blessing that Pindar wrote

for the whores who were welcome
at Aphrodite's Corinthian shrine

one hundred girls in all
whom a certain Xenophon of Corinth
   contributed

and he also commissioned the poem

in which it says

"in necessity's hand all is becoming"

figure that one out,

in any event

you said to me
"I love you"

and so we found ourselves
   given over to the goddess

the goddess who couples couples,
impossible coupling as well,

for all coupling's impossible

and that's the lesson—

that death is our weakness and strength

except that it's possible,
again as Pindar put it,

to align oneself with the god
in this case a goddess

which is to say

to kiss your two little tits

30.

After the heat the cold comes on

or put it this way:

the whore in me
and the whore in you—

that same openness

that same metaphysical forgery

there is in a name and beyond all candor

doesn't leave a thing behind it

but snowy emptiness

I said—
I'm looking for a vacant heart

in order to run
     wild within it

one can see how cold is produced
to produce heat

that heat is the violence
          of coldness

Bubellah
your coldness, your coldness
is what drew me

because the
two of us need

heat so badly

I believed without really knowing it

that the cold
would suck up all the heat

but ran
into a steppe of snow

like the Baron of Munchausen

and little by little
it's becoming clear

that my true partner
        in love

is the hairy behind of your husband

that you're
a bizarre animal with a bodily

hump—
a kind of sphinx

with the face
of an angel, an angel, an angel

and, on the other hand,
hermaphroditic organs

though spiritually too—

because you're condemned
        for all eternity
to betray words

betrayal— you'll tell me—

which is their pathos
(and so my own and yours)

that's the hell of words
which is the hell of love ...

like Dante
I pass by and look on
    with a shudder

as a black demon

rises within the mire
of the body, of time, of meaning

clasps your belly
            in his arms

whereas I'm forced to go on

and so
cause you to dwindle

to dwindle
like a comet in space

you're
a word on a printed page

but the writing draws
all its vitality from you

who said: "I love you"

and then was torn like a star

out of herself, out of her words

and from here on in
these words will hang in space

empty but waiting
        for a soul

and meanwhile sustaining themselves

on other words, compassionate neighbors,
on anticipation, hope, and faith

under the aegis of God

31.

In the dark you tell me
(referring to your husband)

"And they shall be
one flesh"

and from this flesh
flesh is formed

the fact of which is hedged
in the holy letters: LOVE
    (*A-Ha-Ba-H*)

Aleph—Elohim (God)
Hè—HaShem (The Name)

and the letter Bet
Briyah (Creation)

Brit (the Covenant)
and again Hè—

to remind you of HaShem
            (The Name
in case you've forgotten)

"Come on Aharon
and be The Name

to defend myself
from myself

(for only the self
is the self's enemy)

I'll strip utterly

until I'm transparent

and you'll
inseminate me with the word

and no one, no one's more beautiful
                than I am

for I've already stepped
out of myself

and become your beauty

I'm the crown of your poems

me, D., in you
and you know

what D. is in 'I' (*Ani*)
and what I will be

when D. finds room
(between A and N: *ADoNoI,* the Lord)

for you've written the Song of Songs

for in fact you thought
you were the monster

(that Sphinx)
but that's the confusion

that's the unholy
mix of The Name

man and woman
a beast

a rapacious lion

its prison the holy
    letters

as was said: Aleph
and the same: Hè
and the same: Bet

and again: Hè

and the prison is me entirely—
The Name, my name
when D. is in me

who guards your self
against yourself

(because only the self
is the self's enemy)

and you strip before me
    utterly

become transparent

and there's no longer anything more beautiful
                        than you
for you've crossed the threshold

and become my beauty—

the splendor
of those same legs

which are written with Aleph
and the other letters of the Name
                    as above

which guard, as I said,
myself from me
yourself from you

and so you have it—a writ—

your writ is your right

your contract in marriage

and now read, and don't die"

4.

I want to lie in wait for you
within these details

to listen wait until its so wait

and, suddenly,
simply to snatch you away

behind
by that deep gesture

that deep gesture
which was, as it were, created just
so that it's escaped

the hand would slip

and then again
the curve holds your body, a smooth
as another adopted

and the body's triumph
...and smooth because of my touch

...how I until life
how will I go back to live

and how will I build you

Additional
Poems

i.

Tithonos married the goddess of dawn

Eos
and when he was old
    she left him

imprisoned in a palace
near the sea

and there he cries for eternity

and Peleus knew Thetis
who gave birth to Achilles

—she had legs of silver
and he too was abandoned
(and his son killed at Troy)

and I want a bowl
of oatmeal

not a goddess, but you

as though I'd said:
I'm reduced
  to a slice of bread—

not a goddess, but you

and a bowl of oatmeal

ii.

I'd like to be your slave

I've never once felt

how fully the slave is the true master
mostly what I want is to care for your body

to bathe it
to trim your nails

also to brush your hair

to wash it
and clean your cuts when you're cut

(for I myself am now a cut)

with my finger I'll wash the spaces
between your toes

I'll help you when you get the runs
and during your period

you'll come out of the bath, your flesh steamy

and I'll give my being
over to your clothes exclusively

all my attention to your bra and your panties
your damp towel and your skirt ...

and I can tell you:
these are the clothes of my truth

iii.

In every conceivable form of existence

I'll fuck you

(be you goddess, human, whore, or beast)

Periandros the King killed his wife
Melissa, and afterward slept with her

it was all revealed in a dream
in which she appeared and hinted at the act

she asked him for clothes
(because she was cold in the grave)

and he stripped the women of Corinth
and in her honor burned their dresses

in any event this hint
(to prove to her husband Melissa was speaking)

was: "You've put your bread in a cold oven"

(meaning the sperm
and the cunt of the murdered woman)

the impossible distance between us
I too, I too call death—
So what?

Should I set up a statue of you in my bed,
like Admetos?

How can the living fuck the dead?

iv.

You've emptied my life

Now I'm always tapping my feet
impatiently, waiting

and I can't work

sex to me is worthless

because I've learned what a goddess is—

it's the unattainable woman
(the attainable through that which can't be attained)

I'm stuffed with the tedium of a star

now that I'm severed from all earthliness
my element here is space

and I encounter the various bodies

and treat them in accordance with the ethics of space,
                    the camaraderie of space

with the joy of the "boundless", the empty—

as one star to another

V.

I'd like to touch you

it would be splendid to touch a thought

and be convinced of its corporeal essence
(a pleasant, juicy corporeal essence)

and, on the other hand, this unified flesh
(the body, whose unity is its love— my love)

is, in the process, scrambled into thoughts
                        and words
into a chain of problems and stories

it populates earth and sky

and grasps with ropes or reins

all the horses of being

buckets and buckets of muddy cement

are, in this manner,
attached to my despair

to the paradise which is your armpit

and this link is alive
for it's fact—we're walking around inside it
it drives us

and it walks within and before us

as a pillar of fire, as pillars of fire

it also takes care of the stragglers

so that pits and pits of clay

carcasses we flay in the market

are immediately conscripted as soldiers
along the erotic crusade

my mind holds them like pliers
and won't let them betray us
(even if my mind is nothing less
    than them and them again)

and they'll set sail
despite all the academic committees,
the obstacles on every path

toward the land that's holy

because that's the direction— the meaning—
                of the entire dictionary

(and a dictionary's never anything in itself,
    never neutral,

but always a body and of a body) he says

I'd like to touch you

vi.

So long as I don't fuck you

I'm filled to the brim
and remain full

and stand before your life
like a seraph

"the appearance of brightness,
as the color of electrum"

electrifying actually

threatening actually
to bring about marvelous changes within you

to bestow upon you
vitality rhythms and meanings

though all this ground—
a plot of a kind of Mother Earth—

is rendered
not of this time and not of this place

and an artificial desert is formed
wherein you stand, like Pasiphae,

a charming and beautiful girl
who lost her mind and fell in love
    with the bull of Minos

(she was that same king's wife)

Daedalus the crafty, the artist

placed her nude
within a model cow

he constructed of planks
and probably planed and smoothed

so that the marvelous pure-white bull
which burst forth from the sea as a gift from Poseidon

that god-like bull
with which at the moment I identify

wouldn't wound its testicles

when it bent its huge body
and thrust its maleness
into that work of art made of wood

that artificial cunt
across which exists

the warm natural cunt of the woman

and these are the two sisters
(art, let's say, and life)

and without crossing through one
there's no reaching the other

vii.

Does love belong
to life ever after?

Is love
all that we lack?

And maybe the inverse is better—

that everything at hand is love,

that all, as in Parmenides,

is one huge lump
that knows nothing but love

and that hate, that deficiency

are games of hide and seek

within an economy

of material which is always power,

pervasive and always in labor—
giving birth (at every location)

and the hatreds and betrayals

adorn us like flowers
with which, at the delta,
          (The Nile's)

the girl who turned
into a cow was adorned—

Zeus's lover— Io ...

when I think of Io
I want to smell your sex

yes, to lift up
the hem of your skirt

and look at that flower

a kind of lily
in the bush of its hair—

its petals set at the tip of your belly

I'm well aware
this is divine geography

that the navel is Delphi—
        Omphalos—the navel

that in the vulva the gods are concealed

that the legs are the model

for all standing, all direction, all elevation
                and progress

the legs are the way toward
in any event
I lower my head like a pilgrim

and think, as I mentioned, of Io—

she was a girl

her father a river and King of Argos

and on her bed she heard Zeus whisper

from behind the wall
"Come, you'll like it,

come out with me to the meadow
beside the spring of Lerna ..."

and now I'm changing my mind

and know that love is power indeed

only power, only power, only power

and much like Zeus
with lightning I'd threaten your husband and father

and open-mouthed
they'd send you

to me—out to the grass and the mud

for he who has no lightning in hand
let him stay away from love

let him open a grocery store,

sweetheart
come, come out for me to the spring of Lerna

like Io
agree to become a cow

agree to be ravished

for fate is always

violation and change—

which is to say, to love—

which is to say—
to be a god

sweetheart, you'll have to become a cow

if you don't want to be less than a woman

viii.

The distance between us, it's becoming clear

writes across you
changing your face

and you're less pretty
than you might have been

because the Lord

works through messengers

and each such messenger
  is the good beekeeper

responsible
for a certain number of bees

in a given corner

it's sad to see

the neglect in my hive

we should sever the hands of people
who tamper with honey and nectar

I'm mumbling now
(though I also know

that they too will be thought of as bees

in need of a keeper ...)

so you, my sweet,

up to your neck in the mediocre

"You don't blame me"—
        you say, hoping—
and these words also

remind me of when I was young
(on Kibbutz Merhaviya)

and the horse Ruhama—

the idea being
that a man's no different than a beast

to wit—
he needs to be thoroughly scrubbed
        "within and without"

and scraped down with a strigil

and even
reigned in with a bridle

of patent leather

Ach, how I'd bridle you

and how I'd run that lazy blood

within your limbs

because you've sunk, sunk in the mire of marriage

what stinking hay, my sweet,
you're eating ...

That's it,

the distance here is the real hero

see how his teeth are stuck in

and resemble the contours
of the various continents
the hand that shapes

(these torn parts)

also prompts
the longing, the yearning—

the best of dreams

are, after all, spun on the loom of distance

but band-aids, too, and dressings,
    saying you're sorry and lying,

Oh bubellah
on your lips which are what
  above all I crave

moles of lying grow

ix.

A cow gives milk

the hen's gift—
        an egg

an idiot
asks of the cow an egg

or
with greedy hands

looks for a teat
on the hen;

you fool,
go skip in the thistles

and get out of my hair;

all of the above
concerning myself:

I imagine you

born of the sea-foam,
curves upon curves,

and ahh, what legs!

If I
had several members

my desire would never
say enough ...

What a fool,

I thought we'd meet

holding maps
of two different planets
        in our hands

you said—

I love you

I took my bag
and went to meet you

but you were talking
Indian-talk

and in Indian-talk
love's

a playful tickle
around the navel

and nothing more,

a tickle

and after
you turn on your bum

and light a fire

or fuss with the kettle

indeed—

a playful thing

I didn't understand

"I love you"

was only a story

the story— not about me

but about yourself

and a story is always
a story spun out of (within) a story

someone else is speaking

I'm thinking of Philomela

whose brother-in-law raped her
and tore out her tongue

and she wove a pattern
into a piece of cloth

her story in glorious colors

and became in the end a nightingale

which is to say, like you,
she told a story with a bob of her tail

—that tail I don't mean to belittle

(in fact it's all I can manage,
        and long, to catch hold of

like the rest of the world ...)

A man full of desire and full of words

I'm gazing
with blinking eyes at my cloth

I've told a story about myself,

and in the end
what's left of me? A tail

SELECTED POEMS

1966-1995

TEACHERS' ROOM

1966

BEFORE SCHOOL

Before school
I was out with the low trees,
the radishes and green onions,
in a small garden, dawdling.

In a canvas hut, before I came
they'd put out several benches.
The sun crawled over the tablecloth's plaid,
a hand touched down, and turned to milk
standing in a pitcher and cup.

KIBBUTZ

1973

II. OUR CULTURE

Our culture's contained in a few
tools and their objects—
i.e., a straw broom,
a chisel,
a pitchfork and scoop,
caustic soda
for the calves' horns,
a rubber pipe, a glass
tube and inseminator's glove.

A battery
set in a wheelbarrow
covered with burlap
beside a fence in the pasture.
A system of swinging gates,
barriers, and rails
to guide the cattle,
a hooked rod
for catching chickens,
a beak clipper
and carbolic
acid sprayer
to disinfect the woodwork.

A hoe
stuck at the end
of a row of beets,
or safflower,
beside the path that cuts
across the fields of corn
and staked tomatoes,
passing through
an olive grove
to sorghum tracts and vetch

near the hay press and harrows,
a seed plow—
in a can beneath
its perforated seat,
pitchers of soup and lemonade
aluminum plates,
a tin of chopped meat.
A vegetable garden's
wheel-hoe,
a potato combine,
a pyramid of crates,
sacks,
and rubber baskets.

A stack
of light pipes
and hammer sprinklers,
a wrench
to tighten the fit
of the pipe
to the nozzle.
A pick-axe,
its helve braced
with a strip of wood,
the plumber's tripod
and some flax,
minium,
rubber gaskets,
a pump
in a metal shed
locked
beside
a beehive.

A hammer
wet from watering
the prefab concrete parts,

a hand saw,
2 and 4 inch nails,
boards
piled up between
angled iron struts
or beams,
stuck in upright,
iron
rods calibrated—
simple, rolled—according
to the ceiling's weight
and column's height ...

IV. THE DINING HALL

I like the potato
peeler

the bread slicer

and the two huge pots with the steering
wheels on the side

the storeroom for crates

I like the kitchen in its entirety

including the loading dock's concrete floor

a tractor approaches and lowers a pig in a wash-tub

I've often gathered up packing material

I like the convenience
of egg cartons

a broken egg in one of the thirty
depressions constructed of pulp

a can with the crumbs of cookies

garbage doesn't repulse me
I like the concept "eating"

and "eating together"

in a building called The Dining Hall

mornings a cook and staff on-duty

just released from the army

renew the procedures of cooking and serving

in an alcove one of the women
members attends
to a boiler

I remember a morning like this:
I was sent to the carpentry shop to get sawdust
and scattered it near the entrance

a young woman
on her way to breast-feed aroused me

the dining hall's built on a hill
beneath which shelters were dug and serve
as storerooms for times of emergency

at the back of the hall
pipes, drains
crates on some tall metal shelves

I like all kinds of materials

the metal with which a tray is made,
the metal with which a fork is made,
the metal with which a strainer is made,

wood's exploited to make a large spoon,
the haft of a knife,

a dough trough, a pastry board,

the rim of a sieve and a whisk's handle

I like gas

I like electricity

I like cooking salt

The kibbutz eats salad

I'm standing beside
a small stainless steel table

slicing some herring

and white cheese

I'm thinking
I need to wash off a plate

there's a slice of uneaten bread on a plate

after lunch one has to wash
each utensil

a pot in which the main course was cooked

the gridwork lifts out of the floor by the drain

I was told
to take a pail full of apples

out of the electric ice box

I was told I needed to peel some vegetables

I carried a crate
of green peppers
out of the storeroom

I took out a trash can

of onion skins

In the sink I soaked some radishes
in another sink I soaked some carrots

I soaked plums

in a metal container in the store room is rice

food concentrate and expensive items
are stored there too

dried food
like oats for porridge

all sorts of legumes

the window's darkened by a bush outside

in the cupboard sweets are kept
with various syrups

a large quantity
of coffee, cocoa, and tea

a sack of white cloth full of raisins rests
beside

a sprayer
that works on air pressure

a shoulder strap is screwed
into the tank

meat's brought in
on a wagon

from the cold room near the silo

meat in a sack

there's a small ramp
in the room they've set up
a barrel for water

the tap and sink are outside

VII. EDUCATION

1.

The first thing I think of
is suffering, even an insult
some kind of sorrow

emotional involvement

the thing from which
I've always fled

2.

the thing I need
to think
a thought
that's honest or
so that every
value might be valid

3.

and it's impossible
without it
to build a factory well

impossible

to found a kibbutz
I feel an institution

4.

A construction company
workers' library

out in the fields
beside
an abandoned airstrip

a party activist
riding a donkey

toward the clubhouse at Shunem

5.

I'm thinking of
a bakery
called Our Daily Bread

that made rye bread
(during the days
of the Mandate)

How are you
workers of Our Daily Bread?

6.

I feel
an education

each book
entailing
gratification's delay

not to flee,

to understand.

Each book,
geometry too,
also "Knowing the Land"—

the classroom's a poignant place

somehow I felt
I, Aharon, was a closet (*aron*)

a modest closet

a closet's
a cultural tool

the hanger
implying the clothing

7.

Education needs to encourage
feeling

in a notebook one should read
and write of love

but not ignore
sloth and negative feelings

one has to study
every fact
with detachment that really exists

a number's marvelous
in numbers there's great possibility

a marvelous compass
a compass of wood and a smaller
compass of tin

the blackboard's a marvel
smooth and square, a black slate
a green slate
marvelous chalk
marvelous writing utensils
a pencil, a pen

electricity inside the classroom
is turned on only in winter

water's outside

only the lab
has water inside it

in first grade
one learns to write
writing in pencil
one learns to add

one talks and sings of the seasons
of the different
kinds of rain

for the first time in an active way a person encounters a book

and one learns to spell
the names of certain important pieces of furniture
a desk, a chair
the spelling of pronouns,
of certain positions,

one learns how to use the Hebrew vowels

one learns division

there's a risk involved in spelling
aggression inside the word
vetch
fear in the words
division, Arab

I learned
about transportation

I learned
about Tel Aviv

The Bible's fantastic
especially fantastic from a distance
that's real

an elderly teacher
from Denepropetrovsk
taught us the Bible

a teacher who always
had eczema
on her hand

I'm using
a secular language

I love what's alive
and what's present
I love activity

I love the word industry

I love
the words

agriculture, agricultural

I studied literature
and poetry
I studied history

Down below,
half a mile or so from the classroom
the *Altalena* was shelled
during a lesson

and we lay on the floor
listening
to the shooting

the school had no
psychologist
a doctor came
to give us shots
a nurse
saw to hygiene

true
hygiene comes
only with self-awareness

the nurse
was Dov Sadan's
sister-in-law

the school had a regular dentist

a cleaning woman
lived in a structure beside
the basketball court

the school had an office

science is studied
in the garden and lab

in the lower grades one's taught to rake

I saw
a wooden plow
one discusses
horse manure and chicken shit

on the kibbutz one hunts for a buzzard

in the field one finds a swamp cat

one shoots at a bird
from within a boat on the fish pond

each class has a house of its own

in each such house there are
six rooms and each room
has four beds
the closet has compartments
and a shelf for every child

at the end of the hall there's a classroom
at the other end are the toilets and showers

there's also a bathroom just for the counselor

above each towel
there's a label for names

extra clothes
are kept in the basement

there's another common storeroom for bikes

a shack where bedspreads are woven

the dining room's a larger shack
imported from Sweden or Germany

the students get seedlings of buffalo grass

the students get chemicals

the students get a fetus preserved in formaldehyde

the students are given a room for taxidermy

the students are given a painted sink
plugged with stencils

the students are given drafting boards

the students are given a steel stylus

the students are given a scraper

the students are given acid, oxygen, headphones

radio crystal, a magnet, shovel, syringe

a hunting rifle
a trap, a sack, and glue

a jar, paint, a typewriter

athletic equipment is scattered around in the grove

some of it's kept in a crate:

ropes, nets, a shot put,

a field hockey ball

athletic equipment
is strewn beneath the beds

the expensive equipment is ruined in the rain
the pommel-horse leather is sensitive to dampness

in the institute
a beam is called *senada*
a beam painted at the ends for scouts

from beams they built
an obstacle course
for pre-army training

in the woods
are nettles and tin

a camel foal
was raised and killed by poison there

children keep cages and pets

an older girl, Clara, became
a drill instructor

a child's in charge
of the hives
and runs the well

the janitor's helped
by a teacher-driver

dress is involved
in education—
value's implied by fabric

inferior work
is cause for a fight

the concept of help is developed

in neighborliness
the question of hygiene comes up

the margins of feeling are given
over to politics

a library encourages precision

a library drives us to
play, the body

effort in a book is arousing—

reading's work

work wounds

thirst is formed, fatigue created
the body grows handsome

on the blackboard the teacher has drawn
a testicle

the teacher displays
several means of prevention

love is nourished by giving

THE DOMESTIC POEM

1976

1.

I write

a poetry

free
of ambiguity

my subject

is

a soul
striking root

2.

The subject:
loyalty

the style
fit for thinking

of sacred connections

of love
and of loyalty

3.

of loyalty

of permanence

and continuity

of work

(of house
work
and work outside)

of cleanliness

4.
I see
a piece of furniture

a packed cupboard

in fact a simple

painted wooden crate

called a cupboard

a piece of furniture

5.
and placed in the kitchen

facing
an identical piece

I think
the kitchen contains

an Eden

of wisdom

6.

Wisdom nests
in fire and salt

the water supply
is mythological

nourishment
is another material state of the dream

7.

Bread meat and vegetables
are required for our existence

therefore we buy them
by any means

sometimes at risk
to existence itself

8.

I read a poem by
Alcman on cheese

I too will write
a poem about cheese

9.

Out of necessity
we're nourished

necessity gives rise
to the sweetest

of fruits
nutrition love

10.

Fruit chewed in the mouth

(mentioned by Valéry
in "The Cemetery by the Sea")

orange pulp an acid rich
in Vitamin C

rich in bubbles
of pure saliva
and not at all repulsive

11.

Pure is the word
for mouth

a mouth produces
a word. Speech

("the true secretion
of the mollusc man." Francis Ponge)

12.

A mouth is
an organ of love

and in addition
produces speech

promotes nutrition
absorbs and disseminates taste

13.

I love you

eleven years
I've loved you

six and a half years ago
I took you to be my wife

we're man and wife
undivorceable

14.

We live here
the two of us man and wife
undivorceable

we live here
the two of us man and wife
undivorceable

15.

We have a bed
we have sheets

we have a kitchen table
of unpainted pine

we have a stool
and a sleeping bag

16.

Our values guarantee
that

the object contains

itself

17.

A clean essential utensil

even the substance of the walls

a chair is a wondrous machine

because we wanted
and brought forth a girl

18.

I'm a farmer
of the utensil

I'm sent
to lift a clog

I do the wash I peel

19.

There's an apple in the
southern part of the apartment

the space is divided
to ward off boredom

the frying pan has a handle
to ward off boredom

20.

A needle increases
the value of life

a pin and clock-hand

the sexual organs
are channels of fecundity

21.

Also a radish lying
there

(in the cardboard box
a little damp)

and on the floor
ants and crumbs

22.

On the table
a mix of fruit

on the other hand
on the floor

a dirty shirt

23.

It suits flour
to be spilled

suits each thing
for example: an egg

24.

A winter orange
shines
    like Lorelei

whereas
butter's severe

25.

The sandal

Aeschylus called

a servant
of the sole

26.

I was told the cunt
is full of honey

or

I was told that in the cunt
there's honey

. . .

34.

Silk's secreted
from a worm

I'm an expert
    on eiderdown
soaked with urine

35.

One has to wait
    for a dress

and meanwhile
drink water

36.

Jam's
concocted from quince

at one and the same time
the belly arouses

37.

Remember
our perspective:

to drink water

38.

It's a pleasure
to crush a pair of eyeglasses

sewing a jacket
is epic

39.

A bare leg
beside the vagina

I kiss you
and kiss you
and kiss you

40.

There are
tiny hairs

at the base of the back

41.

Teeth are hard

just as the breast
is soft

42.

A woman without
a saddle

a woman who isn't
a lizard

43.

My muse is
a human vine
a rhetorical nymph

a ravished vine

44.

You create
your ears

and the line
down through your ass

45.

A finger on
a piece of felt

and in the eyes and ears:
                    a trumpet

46.

I'm an archeologist
of your eyeglasses

your life passes
in sugar

47.

You who prefer
  parsley

but I
ground meal

48.

I befriended
  a leek

I—an ambassador
of dough

49.

I admire
      thread

my metaphysic
is air

50.

A steel
Pindaric girder

and a basket of eggs

51.

A shirt's
potential

and to strip
like a mule

52.

I'm a chemist
          of bananas

I vaporize
I secrete
          pepsin

53.

A metallic soul

and also
a checkered cloth

54.

I'm a student
of the chair

55.

I'm the apex
of a triangle

whose base angles
are formed by bread and book

56.

I'm
the common denominator

of bread and shit

58.

Death is
a jacket's absence

BEGIN

1986

in Brisk. She was murdered there by the Nazis. Only a half-dozen men knew about the birth of my daughter Chassiah— it was one of our better-kept secrets. Life in the underground is extremely demanding. It doesn't allow one to share in the grief of mourners or rejoice with those who have reason to rejoice. All that was changed by my daughter. The British, who'd been searching for my wife for years in order to get to me, were looking for "a woman with a child." Now there was a woman with two children. This thoroughly confused them. Where was the woman with the child? They soon lost the trail.

Chassik was born "doubly illegal." I wasn't able to give her my real name, and I couldn't even lend her the name I'd taken on. At the hospital no one was supposed to know that there was such a "Sassover", and that he lived on Yehoshua Ben Nun Street. As the rabbis say: more knowledge, more pain. Nor was I able to go to the hospital to see my daughter. My friend Yisrael Epstein took this difficult task upon himself. He lent his name to my wife and my daughter. The situation was tricky, however, and could easily have led to serious confusion. At the same hospital, at the same time, it turned out that a son had been born to a woman whose name was also (or really) Epstein, and when Yisrael came to the hospital the beaming nurse came up to him and said:

—Congratulations, congratulations, Mr. Epstein, your wife has given birth to a baby boy.

The behavior of this happy "father" surely must have seemed odd to the good nurse. Instead of asking to see his wife and son, he turned on his heels and ran to report the news—that he had a son. Good Yisrael! Afterwards the misunderstanding was cleared up. We were happy, very very happy. The celebration of the "bris," needless to say, would have been too complicated for the overjoyed members of the underground.

But a daughter of Israel deserves a celebration as well. Could a Jew like me, who had the good fortune to be blessed with a daughter, not offer at least a kiddush to the congregation? Obviously a kiddush was called for. My "position" demanded it, it was "obligatory". Therefore, we arranged for a full celebration. On Shabbat I went up to read from the Torah and the good gabbai read the blessing in a lilting voice—and her name in Israel shall be called?

—Chassiah bat Yisrael (Chassiah the daughter of Israel)!

—Congratulations! Congratulations, Mr. Sassover—the Jews said to me, warmly shaking my hand.

—Congratulations, congratulations, Rav Yisrael—said the elderly Rav Simcha. Jewish pleasure filled the small synagogue. And pleasure filled my heart. How grateful I was to the good Jews who had shared in my joy during the time of my seclusion. I stood there, at once moved and a little embarrassed.

With the end of the prayers for the morning, the kiddush was held. Everything had been taken care of. Thanks to the loyal members of the underground, we even had pieces of herring with toothpicks stuck through them. The under-

—from Menahem Begin's autobiography, *The Revolt*

from PART II

47.

"Chassik was born"
    (it says)

and birth

always
  as we know
involves concealment

48.

"Was born" as he put it

"doubly
     illegal"

and indeed it's written—
     "and she concealed him"

49.

The whole business
    of this Hebraism

is
that concealment in birth—

to lend
an ear to what's been born

50.

And "the Hebrew midwives"

(to whom
the king of Egypt speaks)

are in fact
the Hebrew that gives birth

51.

And what's hidden
          in birth?
(the word birth: *laydah*)

we ask

although
this is a question a fool would ask

52.

The Lord
is hidden in birth—

(I say, not
without being

aware of it sounding
as though I'd just
laid a fart)

53.

Which is to say—

first of all

    that Yah

whose grammatical function is
in addition

54.
The birth within

I call it

and the Mekhiltah
writer's example is:

55.
The *yod* (the 'y')
Yehoshua received

    or the *hey* (the 'h')

Abram and Sara took on
when they were opened
    to THE NAME

56.
And were given birth
in other words, were given a name

and the name (*HaSheM*)
is their There (*HaShaM*)

57.

"Invisible
       (in his action)

like the soul"

it says
(in the Midrash on
       "The Life of Sarah")

58.

Except that it's revelation

(in that same
       being concealed)

is also in
the letters 'y' and 'd'
       (*yod* and *dalet*)

59.

The same strong
       hand (the *yad*)

which brings us out
and when the letters
       are reversed
it's revealed
(is born)
as *d'ay*: ENOUGH

60.

For indeed the word

Jew (*Yehudi*)

is a joining

of *yah* and *d'ay*

61.
And once again
a circle is drawn

(around
that newborn child)

and we've returned
to the issue
of the Lord *(shadday)*

62.
"I am the Lord thy God"—
    El Shadday
    it says

meaning
(according to Rashi)

I'm the one-of-whom
(in whom) there is
enough *(sh'd'ay)*

63.
There is, indeed,
enough

and that is
is enough

and there's enough
of this 'is'

64.

meaning
(in *is*, in *enough*)
        the newborn child

(who has enough

and is itself enough)

65.

And this indeed
is the breast's
firmness
(its message)

and we'll
return to this

. . .

96.

"I wasn't able"
    (it says)

to give her

my real name"

97.

"I couldn't even

lend her the name
I'd taken on"

and that marvelous Yisrael—

98.

Yisrael Epstein

"my brother my soul"
    he

calls him
running around in his way

99.

to the hospital and back

    and even

out of excitement presenting
himself as the child's father

100.

("Your wife has given birth
    to a baby boy"

he was told

because

of some other Epstein)

101.

For it's
no longer possible

to return
to the father—
to the source

(if one doesn't
want to become a degenerate)

102.

Because the direction
(the meaning)

is forward—

TO BE
A FATHER YOURSELF

103.

And to return
    to the father

        means

to sink
into illusion and dreams

104.

and in the end
to reduce

to be a thwarted,
mimicking ape

. . .

111.

And The Name
is otherness—

a metonymy

of The Name (*HaShem*)
is The Breast (*HaShad*)

112.

"And therefore
all of Israel's wisdom

let's put it this way,
in short,
'on one leg'

is
The Breast's Wisdom
    (its study)"

113.

And so Pharaoh's daughter too

grew desperate

　　and they were forced

to rush
the child's mother in

114.
It didn't work out
with the Egyptian nursemaids

　　because

The Lord
"made their teats unfit"

115.
And she (Yochaved)
nursed

(him) for two years

it says
"24 months"

116.
And this, for her,
　　was "enough"

　　and so

in nursing
one first of all gives "enough"

117.

Again,
the milk isn't

what's essential

but the *enough*

118.

And to discover
in the newborn child

that "enough" (which is enough)

and, as in a mirror,
that enough—within "the self"

119.

And all this
is *midrash*

but nothing

will prosper
without
adherence in practice

120.

Don't worry
then

about the
world's repair

but (first of all)
brush the nipples

121.

(prior to birth)
with a kind of towel
    and it's important

(so the skin won't crack)

to avoid
using any soap

122.

You create
    with your fingers

a kind of "v"

and nurse him
with the nipple

123.

For meanwhile
the baby's been born

    and there's no point

in waiting around

124.

He's prepared
        to suck

    at once

or the reflex takes a while
(some twenty minutes)

125.

Nurse—
nurse at once

and you'll free
yourself

more quickly
from the placenta

126.

And put in
        not only the nipple

but the whole

tip of the breast
(the dark round of flesh)

127.

Within
3-5 minutes

you'll feel a tickle

and the milk will spurt

128.

At first
it's only a drip

    through

those lactic capillaries

129.

One disposes,
too, of

the black caca
    (the meconium)

if
you nurse at once

130.

And that's thanks
    to the colostrum

the feces quickly yellows

becomes a kind
of split pea stew

131.

And the odor's reasonable
(at one and the same time

   the danger

of jaundice
decreases)

132.

And remember
you're granting him

(in every sense—
nutritionally
and in terms
   of digestion)

the ideal food:
MOTHER'S MILK!

133.

You're granting
   (as I said)

mother's milk!

On the other hand, remember,
you're not a restaurant—

134.

You grant

life

warmth

continuity
insight, and gentleness

135.

You've always nursed
(this child)

and always will

go on nursing
but that nursing

136.

differs
each time
in concept

and will be
internalized
(in the child

who'll become
a man and father)

and so
is maintained

137.

Food on the whole

(as a concept)

is allegorical

food
is what disappears

138.

(disappears in the mouth,
in the blood

in the stomach

in the intestines
in the brain)

139.

So that the essence
    of food

is the level
at which
        it disappears—

the level to which
one lifts it

140.

And this, indeed,
the mother knows:

she determines

the levels at which
the milk disappears

141.

She guides
the milk

and, at once,
creates
the meaning (the content)

142.

And the axiom is

that milk
always comes

is always ready
always possible

143.

And the gist of the matter is
because

the milk is suitable
and quickly digested

the nursing is
(more)
    frequent

144.

Nurse often

(give)

(teach giving
teach acceptance

teach taking)

145.

and at any rate
    at least

every two hours

for if
the breasts swell
       (and harden)

146.

there's pain involved

and, on the other hand,
the more frequent the feedings

the more
milk there'll be

147.

All the pain
recedes

    there's

less fear
of blockage

(in one of the
      lactic capillaries)

148.

And there's no need
to weigh (the child)

A simple criterion
     is:

6-8
wet diapers (a day)

149.

He needs to gain
    roughly

120
grams a week,

but
forget it!

150.

First of all
   let him be

like Hannaniah
Mishael and Azariah

for
the milk is holy

151.

It doesn't
       come

to fatten man

to grant him
only sinew and bone

152.

If you will—
       the milk

is what
       you make (of it)

in the sense of

"I will be
what I will be"

153.

Think what
    the milk is

where to guide
    the milk

and from where
(it comes)

154.

Which is to say
think essence:

essence,
manner, purpose

purpose—which is manner
manner— which is essence

155.

The milk
is what matters

and what we think

and here we've spoken
of that same
         breast's wisdom

156.

Begin's
love is marvelous,

It says

"I stood there
moved and a little embarrassed."

157.

"How grateful I was"

he says

"to the good Jews

who'd come to share in my joy"

158.
—several members
of the congregation—

and they were treated

to sliced herring ...

DIVORCE

1990

1. The Car

I've put all my belongings into the back of the car
right now, in fact, I live in the car
I have money for gas
and a wide glass windshield
I take care of the tires and inflate them
then set out in search of a mate

3. A Street

The street's defined as something outside
two rows of buildings
the buildings provide an encasement for families
and I who deserted my family
cut off from the vertical and all that ascends
have no place now in volume at all
I'm one with the god-of-horizon

9. "The last year of my marriage"

The last year of my marriage reminds me of a porch
in the small town of Rishpon, I passed by chance as a child
it was almost evening a middle-aged farmer and farmer's wife
were sitting on chairs (the man was wearing a gray casquette)
and two huge sacks of peanuts rested between their knees

10. Spoon and Fork

The spoon and the fork are a couple
that lives in peace and won't divorce
the spoon doesn't ask the fork
to stand aside and look on
while the newborn emerges and the placenta slips out
and the fork doesn't beat off
on the kitchen table
while the other members of the household are sleeping

14. The Prayer Book

For years I've wanted to write a prayer book
Why? Because I've learned
that the solid hangs upon nothingness
Because I've found that the sentence is a kind of petition
And because I've found that in all that I've said,
in all that I've said I've said only thank you
so, little by little,
                  in fact I've written that book
and today it weighs some two-hundred pounds
and soon it will celebrate its fiftieth birthday
and yesterday I bought it shoes

17. "Sometimes a step"

Sometimes a step
or two from a bathroom door
the scent of my brother wafts up to my nose
someone has a mother
who makes him identical dishes
bread with slices of tomato and cucumber
french toast, latkes, or meatballs
it *is possible* his digestive juices are similar
even if he's ugly, albino, or a stranger
and nevertheless he sends up to my nose
the odor of Ya'akov, my brother

19. The Heart

I'm on my way back from Jerusalem
with my heart split open
I have a two-and-a-half year old son
in the dark of the hall he stopped and said hi
to my face behind the glass
where I stood in the dark on the porch close to the window
the sewer cover under my shoes like a Roman coin
again he said hi
and I turned into a brown horse with a black cock
that would soon disappear into the treetops,
which are really Satan's hair,
understand that my learning and gift
are, by nature, erasure
my son, my son, that's what my love can offer you

20. The Onion Basket

On the iron door in the kitchen
a basket hung
for years I bent a knee before it
gathering the skins of onion
that fell between the gaps in its weave
it doesn't seem right to throw out an old basket
just because it can't keep in
all it holds, apart from its essence
for what is essence if you have neither husk nor floor?

21. "Masha, my mother"

Masha, my mother, swallowed a crown
she locked herself into the bathroom once or twice
and with some pointy object poked around
in the bowl full of stools.
From those good old days behind the door
I hear that click click click—
it's fantastic that each object and purpose contains
a difference which becomes an addition:
the fruit of that clicking is diligence and that's the crown

42. "I tossed and turned"

I tossed and turned half the night
but not over Helen's thighs
it was money trouble that chased the sleep from my eyelids
Would I be able to find a director or dean
to give me back the teacher's gown
and an income
Worry in legend is likened to a stone
rolling along a slope
that stone is a piece of a star
the star singes the lids of my eyes with its light
if I stop worrying darkness will spread through the world
so let me retrace my steps: worry, a stone, a star
these are the stages of worth's awareness
and all work is a worship of fortune and stars

43. To My Daughter

for Lotem

I tried to explain to my daughter
that a person depends on his income
I told her—even the eagle
resembles the man selling pretzels
on the corner of Hess and Allenby Streets
in order to properly love
I have to have something to sell
to see to the state of my beak
which Homer called: "a fence of teeth"
and, downtown, an old Arab once told me:

only a man who stands on his own two feet
grows the third in between, twice as sweet

45. The Shoe

The shoe contains like a spoon
something sublime and above it
this sublimity can't be measured
and yet it has to be shod
it strives to set foot
and all of the body and spirit's ideas
stake their claim in standing and stride
although one could, it's true, go barefoot
into the thistle field of the factual
but ethic and study call for a sole
to ward off injury and leave a trail
the shoe has a certain responsibility
to, and for, all it steps on
and it's best that it stay small—
may we know when it's right to remove it
let us not make it of iron or gold

52. The Door

My neighbor's musical instrument of choice is the door
at first I thought it a major nuisance
and then I saw it was really part
of a kind of percussion sonata
and the aggravation dissolved: now I observe
how skillful this soloist is in his entrance and exit

55. Honor

All my life I've pursued the truth
from failure to failure
and come to resemble the tangerine pulp
my father used to spit out
and so from the bottom of the bowl I'd say:
the truth of the truth was a lie
its specific courage was fear
and there was also another banner: ignorance
ignorance in respect to proper usage
for man was born to use
and usage is setting things up aright
but not on the side of truth—on the side of honor
while in fact we're forced to go on
waving the same old banners
but still, to the figure peering out from the womb
I offer an alternate value—honor
the main thing, I say,
is to seek out what's stable and stand up straight
the fate of man on earth
the end of man, as I see it, is this: to find honor
my friends, a new era is underway:
on the blushing helmet at the penis's tip is written: Honor

ZIVA

1990

1.

Two or three months apart
and I'll save up all my seed for you
I'm the sentry of Ziva's seed
and then I'll fly on the giant plane
like a courier come with a pearl from Luxor
I'll carry the seed in its soft, muscular vessel
toward the Delta of Ziva

3.

I'm obliged to honor your cunt with my tongue
like the prophet who swallows the scroll
and Gideon's soldiers who kneel and lick
the poet talks only of things that he tastes
each taste in his mouth comes to innocence
he builds a tall fence against all that's coarse
and coarseness fades from the coarse;
as Pindar put it, his task is to guard like a dragon
the muses' apples, and the apples given at the gods' wedding,
he has only to bow his head in humility
between his beloved's thighs
as his mouth bestows on her cunt a dewfall of kisses

4.

I pay no attention to the birds' migration
only to the fact that your panties are gone
just now I'm reading how Democritus the wise
has nothing but scorn for people like me
who play no role in the state's repair
the ship on which a community sails
education being its keel
art and science its oars
but I just shut the book
for me it's enough that your panties return

7.

Let's join our apartments' openings
    mouth to mouth and cock to cunt
my only garden grows in my ears
    my ceiling's my forehead
I'm fifty years old and don't have a home
    my only windows are my glasses' lenses
so, Ziva, at least let me live in your rear!

8.

The body's our final farm
and on it there's milk, manure, and eggs
a hothouse and pipes for fluids
so climb onto my member and ride
I'm loaded down with seed
take hold of me by the reins
two little bells above my eyes
will set the pace
Ziva, let's not be lazy, let's hurry and sow
before the sky goes dark
and we hear the caws of the crow

11.

Ziva,
when will I touch the pair of sparrows nesting there in your lap?
I'm arguing now with the purists, those drinkers of chilled white wine
I prefer the beverage that issues straight from your mouth
or at the end of the month, when the gluttonous penis
descends to your pussy, gets dirty with jelly and drunk with must
not even Magellan travelled as far as the heart and mind
moving between the holes of the cunt and bum
and with me that route is daily bread,
like the Centaur who took Deianeira over the river
my fate follows the path I take with my tongue
Basho climbed Mt. Kashima
and left for posterity the full moon
while I'll bequeath to the world
a diamond of spit I've set in your omphalos, Ziva

13.

I brush the teeth of the beast inside me
over the course of twenty or thirty years I've learned
that the role of man is to care for that beast,
the soul doesn't need our attention,
nor does wisdom and art,
one need only stick the pitchfork in
and, with affection, raise the hay to the mouth
therefore, whenever I hear Bach or Mozart,
I say:
Listen, Ziva's pissing!

18.

The essence of wisdom is keeping it short
wisdom's the place where one shuts the book
if anyone asks me about the way
whether I tell them or not doesn't matter
the only way is the way up Ziva's thigh
and all the others will cheat you
let the philosophers go to their libraries
let the poets go to where beans are sold
I'll parade, again and again, over that knee
Aesop's fables a song in my head—
the crow, the donkey, the lion and monkey,
they know how to be still when they enter the vineyard

22.

I pound my egghead hoping it will tell me
why I love your buttocks so
for years I sat in the National Library
reading the chapters of Plato's Republic
and all that I read led me on
from one good thought to another and better
for each I found the proper material
I fathered children and cleaned their caca
bought a house and planted a vine
wrote a book and raised up students
in short, I could have just turned my head
and found the signpost beneath my back
instead of marching for twenty-five years
in order to get to the rear

24.

The pig reads nothing
no academic gown could make it happy
for him it's all a matter of food
(in fact he once devoured
my daughter Nanno's glasses
which had fallen into his pen)
I, too, am a kind of pig
and Ziva the only garbage I'll eat,
the only sustaining value I know,
even wallowing in my own shit
my snout still sniffs around to find
   undigested crumbs of Ziva

METAZIVIKA

1992

1.

Like the ant and the seed, the mouse and the cheese,
   my soul is devoured by all it needs.
It's supposed to build itself a glassed-in tower
   from calcium and protein, iron and sugar,
but wants, in fact, only to be swallowed—
   for which its talent is generally known
in the passage from mouth to mouth, and groin to groin.

5.

Through folly which sprouted neither feather nor wing,
   I ended up in an asshole, from which there's no escaping
and, in the middle of my life as though in a dark wood,
   I found myself astray. Now, noon after noon I brood
on my back on a mattress, praying for the purest of thighs
   to hover over my starving mouth, and my ravenous eyes,
for a patch of pubic hair like a golden parachute.
   Hallelujah, I mutter, to my songbird there in the trees—
Come, take me away—to life on the right side of the panties.

10.

Like a butterfly pithed by a pin near its head
   we'll never be able to rise from our bed:
we'll have to gather our air and sky
   into the limits of flesh and eye.

Like the wings of angels in the chorus of heaven,
   the cups of your bra will gradually whiten:
in the belly the river of Eden will split
   into sweat and sperm, piss and spit;

and the tree of life and the tree of wisdom
   will flourish, at the mouth of the rectum ...

16.

My heart's so full of shit,
and that's the quality in me that sings:

Yesterday we fought with shouts
about money and you got hit—

your glasses flew off—
but the day before

I came to you with my tongue
from the ankle up to your ears

an hour and a half or more
(my cock, like the locomotive

in *La Bête Humaine* by Renoir
pulling the mouth and face around and around

—inside, forward and back—
the body rushing it blood

like fire within me and coal);
you screamed, and bit my lip,

like in Herodotus, where the story's told
of the female flying snake

which, as it comes to a climax,
pierces the throat of its mate.

22.

With each passing season and year
　　the heart descends more toward the rear;
with the cock and in the moistened hole,
　　it battles the angel.

Between the legs it gradually lessens
　　the distance from Rome to Jerusalem;
and that wearying struggle might well be
　　an extension of sorts of Thermopylae

where, on a limited field,
　　the meaning of flesh is revealed—
for as long as you're there in the trap
　　the inversion glows in your lap.

Leonidas, too, before the battle
　　was only combing his hair with his soldiers—
and, over Asia and its massive army,
　　a handful of golden hair shone brightly

from three hundred Spartan men whose loins were bare.
　　So, come to that snare—
your hole is a mirror to all
　　and when I've finished licking it well

a splendor will spread through the world,
　　a glamor that will not easily fade—
but we, like Dieneces,
　　"we'll have our fight in the shade!"

24.

Day after day after day I look on while you're lying down
beside me like a low hill, naked, tufts of grass having grown

here and there along its slopes. And beyond that, I'm certain
something's happening: armies are being deployed, Medean and
      Persian;

Xerxes sits on his throne, with a silver cup in his hand,
or a young man is killing his uncles—the boy from Calydon—

in order to give Atalanta the hide of the wild boar;
and maybe there's also a jungle looming, or a desert floor

where the Phoenix emerges or begins to fade in the sand.
Above that most ideal of landscapes I'll never ascend,

I'll never seek out what's clearly beyond
the body on which I've kissed each limb

and day after day after day, as long as my eyes stay open,
they'll graze on that hill, on that back, on that bottom.

28.

When you were twenty, not wanting to miss even an hour
with your lover who was set to leave for Algiers

you faked a serious stomach ache and played the part so well
that you were taken from the studio to Hospital

Hôtel Dieu's emergency room, where, despite your denials,
an overly zealous doctor removed your appendix after he'd put you under.

Now you're asleep, and beside you I'm wide awake, still
thinking about that scar, that pale seal

branded across your belly for love of a distant and different man
who long ago drowned in the sea. Lord, how I envy him

who, packing a bag and adding some books and trousers,
suddenly gets a call and goes to answer.

Again and again I'm tempted to follow the way
he takes along that river, toward L'île de la Cité:

with me he buys you flowers, climbs the stairs to the right ward
and the room that's draped in white, looks around, then moves toward

your bed, and there inside me you're waiting for him, breathless—
and he smothers your smiling mouth, like a pomegranate, in kisses...

THE HEART

1994

CONSECRATION

The floor's three by three. As in a cathedral
with only a single seat, his gaze climbs
along the length of a pipe and toward the sublime
up to a cast-iron organ attached on high to the wall.

The boy, lowering his eyes to where his pants
lie crumpled on the floor in a kind of detachment,
waits for the bowels' thunder, the stench of excrement,
and the stream of water that always splatters his ass.

He sends a hand back around to the hole,
the issue of which he'll never share with a soul
and, like Jonathan dipping his stick into the hive's

comb, he draws to his lips a fleck of the manna,
licks his finger clean, removing the sign,
and rises, utterly pure and alone, like no one alive.

FOR NATIONAL POETRY WEEK 1992

I look at the Prime Minister's face and remember
how cold and hard the wooden seat of the toilet
was during the days of the British Mandate....
Now, two whores—nationalism and religion—

have taken over the country and made a pact
to turn the heart's pasture into a shithouse
and pluck the feathers of Hebrew culture.
A man wakes, and refuses to look in the mirror.

I see three old women, Rebecca, Rachel and Sarah,
in a soup kitchen passing a tooth from hand to hand;
only a little meat is left on the carcass

of that sweet bird that once sang in the window
from its high branch. Chew slowly, hags, the cupboard's bare,
and soon the Hebrew poem will have to blast from the ass.

AGAIN YOU'RE IN PARIS

Again you're in Paris, and my heart's like butter
stuck in its freezer covered with frost.
Outside little hills of hail and gray slush—
the century's coldest and rainiest winter

swoops in from Turkey: streams rush from their beds;
swept-away shepherds drown as brooks overflow;
chicken coops flood; oak branches break from the pressure of snow
and the cows on the hillsides die in their sheds.

I'm trying to speed up the bodies of heaven,
pushing the stars by night and the sun at dawn,
but not so the rains will lessen

or the cushion of whiteness melt and the earth's arm
release the beads of her gilded dress, like a diva,
but so you'll come home, so you'll come home already, Ziva!

FINDING IT HARD TO FALL ASLEEP

Finding it hard to fall asleep, my mind
slips from the day's refuse and manages to find
a trough between the legs of a rider across from me;
it dreams it's plowing into her thick, hairy

muff, the softer down on her lip my clue
to what eluded my stare on its way into
hiding, deep in the recesses of her white groin.
Whoever you are, wherever, I have no way of knowing....

If they opened my head, in its cells they'd find your pussy
which, in my mouth, just now is speaking through me
like a stolen fetish overcoming the thief in his ploy—

it orders you to retaliate, instantly,
and you swallow his cock, taking it into your hand
like a ripe banana to the mouth of a lazy boy....

I'VE ALWAYS MISSED OUT

I've always missed out on the prettiest girls;
only after they've screwed in every hole and position
do they come to me for help with their poems, or a lesson,
and I tell them of Phoinix, whose lips dripped pearls

of wisdom and how, in exchange for the knowledge, he'd usually
get a comfortable bed with sheets of lambskin and, if he were lucky,
hear—in an adjacent tent—Patroklós
making love with Iphis, and Diomêdê with Akhilleus.

So I won't get to sleep with the prettiest girls.
I'll fix their lines, put up with their stupid chatter,
and, late at night, comfort myself as I stick my finger

into my rear then pull it out and know, lifting it up to my nose,
that the biggest, blackest, and totally most mysterious
dick in the world is lying here in this bed writing my poems.

DRENCHED WITH SWEAT

Drenched with sweat from playing, he takes off his pants
and rests in the deep lap of the goddess of love,
a pure porcelain belly without any hair
leading down to the drain with its nickeled lips.

It's good to lie on one's back, to rest one's head,
exhausted, to send a hand down to the groin
and masturbate slowly. His neck rubs up against
her chilly abstract breasts, her knees define him;

in his mind he turns them over and with his tongue
explores the crease where hip folds into hip
and there gushes the infinite spring of her nakedness.

He wants to pierce her, and, to make the invisible real,
he stands there barefoot, his back to the mirror,
then turns and takes a long hard look at his rear.

IF ALL THE WORLD WERE CONTAINED

If all the world were contained in an automat
I'd never choose juice or even hot chocolate,
but what my balls are always craving instead.
Nearly thirty one years have passed in my head

and my spirit's still depressed about having
hesitated when Anna Traphelt crouched over
my face and ordered me to lick her. I may be a madman,
but ever since then my tongue has grown longer

the further that reddish triangle of springy hair
recedes into the distance, as though in Plato's parable
of the cave, from that room at the Hotel Notre Dame,

and, on the horizon, it sheds and takes on form:
just yesterday it seemed like a honeycomb,
and today it's only a star, its sweetness gone.

AH NILI

She was the friend of a friend and had a boyfriend.
My girlfriend had gone away, they'd fought, and I exploited
the opening and ended up in her room in Holon like a bomb.
She was lying in bed, a little sick, and at loose ends.

To my declarations of love and nibbling hands she responded,
but when I went further she seemed ashamed and got mad.
I only stole a few kisses, and she was having her period
anyway. Ah sweet Nili, I'd drag that night

back by the hair if I could. I left in a cab, dejected,
but two hours later I knocked again on your door
(a one story house with a path and patch of lawn)

and somehow you weren't surprised, as though you'd been waiting.
Nili, I think of your beauty lying there in my arms,
my heart aflame, and realer *then* with you than in me now.

NEVER AGAIN WILL I BREAK THAT RECORD

Nili decided in all seriousness to be my girlfriend;
she came to tell me as much at the Hotel Notre Dame,
and there I lost her as well, like a moron.
But I did manage to have her over once at the house of a friend

and, in a bathroom on Rehov HaYarkon, by the sea,
I knelt and washed her delicate feet and her belly
with the same porous sponge that the maids used when
Odysseus told them to rinse off the tables—the slaughter done.

And I managed to sleep with her, in a spasm of tremendous lust:
for one full summer night on a narrow mattress
at my parents' apartment, I fucked her seven times—beads

of sweat like myrrh pouring between our chests:
once, and once, and five times more, our loins on fire.
Ah Nili, never again will I break that record.

HAPPINESS

The rain comes down and rattles the roof's red tiles
and the heart, too, longs to be decently wet.
I'm reading Aristotle again—who says that the good
is that to which all of existence really aspires

and the supreme good, in its way, is like a pastry
one bakes with all earthly matter and savvy
until it rises to a condition that we call happiness,
and a man sits as though sufficient unto himself—

the ring of beloved souls around him as air,
knowing the golden mean between extremes,
and, like me, listening to the sound of the rain,

reading and thinking, at ease in his arm chair—
when his finger finds in his pants pocket a hole,
burrows down to his member, and starts to twirl.

NOTHING WILL COME OF YOU

"Nothing will come of you, you'll print a few poems"
—a teacher who couldn't stand me, Shaya Nir,
who, when he spoke, sprayed spittle at his listeners;
thus, for me, his prophecy from the world of numbers

a lifetime ago. Behind the delicate mesh
of a screen, several pine trees stood in a cluster.
If, in retrospect, I were to judge from the severity
of their elevated view, it seems he was right:

in the course of a decade I've lost two women—
one of whom, with a flick of her back and trembling
shoulder, could overwhelm stones and trees with desire:

and I've printed poems: I've got a sack of them,
like the goatskin sack of Aeolus, a phenomenal treasure,
though in it there's only wind, and, when you loosen it, nothing.

Biographical Notes

AHARON SHABTAI is the foremost Hebrew translator of Greek drama and the author of numerous collections of poetry. Born in 1939 in Tel Aviv, he attended the Tel Nordau School and the Educational Institute at Kibbutz Merhaviya. After his military service, he studied Greek and Philosophy at the Hebrew University, the Sorbonne, and Cambridge, and from 1972 to 1985 he taught Theater Studies in Jerusalem. He was awarded the Prime Minister's Prize for Translation in 1993. The father of six children, he lives in Tel Aviv.

‭

PETER COLE's books include, *Rift*, a volume of poems (Station Hill Press, 1989), *Selected Poems of Shmuel HaNagid,* translations from the medieval Hebrew (Princeton University Press, 1996), and *From Island to Island,* translations from the contemporary Hebrew of Harold Schimmel (Ibis Editions, 1997). The Sheep Meadow Press will publish *Hymns & Qualms,* his second volume of poems, in 1997.